SIMPLE HIP KNIT
SCARVES™

Edited by Kara Gott Warner

HOUSE of
WHITE
BIRCHES
PUBLISHERS
SINCE 1947

Introduction

When it comes to scarves, you can't go wrong. They're practical, compact, and you can whip one up usually in just one weekend. It really doesn't matter what your skill level is because most knitters I know are fans of scarves. We love to make those sweaters and cardigans, but sometimes you're just looking for some comfort that knitting a scarf provides.

On the pages to follow, we present an eclectic mix of scarf patterns. You'll find a generous selection of easy knit and purl combinations, as well as scarves emphasizing rich texture and color. We've got a mix of long skinnies, some chunkies, neck warmers and scarflettes too.

It's true that the right scarf can add dimension and elegance to any wardrobe. Wear them for warmth on a cold wintry day, or accessorize yourself for a memorable evening out.

Get ready, get set and get those needles clicking!

Kara

Kara Gott Warner, Editor

Table of Contents

Wonder & Whimsy,
page 9

The Long &
Winding Road,
page 39

Chain Male,
page 17

Clarendon,
page 21

The Bold & The Beautiful

Make a statement, take a bold move. Look sultry in Slinky, Silky Waves, or make it fun with Wonder & Whimsy. Bold jewel tones of fuchsia, royal and pink will turn some heads. You'll have to fight off the paparazzi in Bryant Park. You know who you are, so strut your stuff.

Slinky, Silky Waves

This sultry skinny scarf, with wavy lace pattern, is the perfect accessory for strutting your stuff.

Design by Lois S. Young

. . . .

Skill Level
◼◼◼▢ INTERMEDIATE

Finished Size
Approx 6 inches wide x 68 inches long, blocked

Materials
- Himalaya Yarn Duke Silk (worsted weight; 100% silk; 225 yds/ 100g per hank): 1 hank black SI-029
- Size 8 (5mm) 36-inch or longer circular needle or size needed to obtain gauge

4 MEDIUM

Gauge
18 sts and 16 rows = 5½-inch x 4-inch rectangle in pat, after blocking.
To save time, take time to check gauge.

Special Abbreviation
Long Twisted Stitch (LT): Insert needle into next st on LH needle, wrap yarn around tips of both ends of needle, then wrap it once more around tip of RH needle. Knit st through original st and wraps.

Pattern Stitch
Silky Waves
Row 1 (WS): Sl 1 (edge st), knit across to last st, end k1-tbl (edge st).
Rows 2 (RS) and 3: Rep Row 1.
Row 4: Sl 1, k3, *[k2tog] 3 times, [yo, k1] 6 times, [ssk] 3 times; rep from * to last 4 sts, k3, k1-tbl.

Rows 5–7: Rep Row 1.
Row 8: LT in each st across row.

Rep Rows 1–8 for pat.

Pattern Notes
Circular needle is used to accommodate stitches. Do not join, work back and forth in rows.

Slip the first stitch of each row purlwise, moving the yarn between the needles to the back before working the next stitch. The last stitch is knit through the back loop (k1-tbl).

Scarf
Loosely cast on 224 sts.

Work [Rows 1–8 of Silky Waves pat] 3 times, then work Rows 1–6 of pat.

Bind off loosely kwise on WS.

Border
With RS facing, pick up and knit 20 sts along 1 short end of scarf. Bind off kwise on WS.

Rep on other short end.

Finishing
Block severely by stretching scarf and pinning it out to required dimensions. Mist with water from a spray bottle, let dry. ●

Wonder & Whimsy

A colorful scarf that's easy to knit in garter-stitch strips. When wrapped around the neck, the pieces fall gracefully for a multicolored dramatic look.

Design by Katharine Hunt

Skill Level
◼◼◻◻ EASY

Finished Size
Approx 6½ inches wide x 72 inches long

Materials
- Noro Iro (chunky weight; 75% wool/25% silk; 132 yds/100g per ball): 4 balls fuchsia, green, brown multi #103
- Size 11 (8mm) needles or size needed to obtain gauge
- Small stitch holders or safety pins

Gauge
7 sts = 2 inches/5cm in garter st.
Gauge is not critical for this project.

Pattern Notes
In order to minimize yarn tangles, begin knitting 3 strips at the same time, then 2 strips and then remaining 2 strips.

After completing the first set of strips, examine the remaining balls and choose the most pleasing color segments to place adjacent to the completed strips.

In garter stitch it is easier to count ridges (2 rows) instead of single rows.

A diagram is provided to help identify strips in each section.

Instructions

Section 1
Cast on 21 sts.

Work in garter st for 3 ridges.

Next row (RS): K3, *[place the next 3 sts on st holder] twice, attach new ball and k3; rep from * once more.

Continue in garter st on strips A, D and G until they measure 22½ inches. Place these strips on stitch holders. Break yarn on strips D and G; do not break yarn on strip A.

Attach new balls of yarn to strips B and F, and work in garter st until they measure 22½ inches.

Rep for strips C and E.

Lay work on a flat surface making sure that all 7 strips are the same length, adjusting if necessary. Break yarn on all strips except A.

Slide all stitches from strip G to A onto a needle, being careful not to twist them.

Next row (RS): Using yarn from strip A, knit across all sts, then work 3 garter ridges, ending with WS.

Sections 2 & 3
Rep Section 1.

Bind off kwise on WS.

Finishing
Block by laying flat and covering with a damp cloth until dry. Do not press. ●

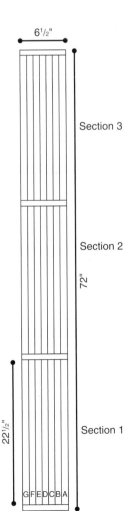

Bryant Park

Worn in a bow or simply wrapped once around the neck, this is the perfect project for small amounts of two lovely yarns in complementary colors.

Design by Ann Weaver

. . . .

Skill Level
■■□□ EASY

Finished Size
Approx 4 inches wide x 50 inches long

Materials
- Blue Sky Alpacas Royal (fingering weight; 100% alpaca; 288yds/100g per skein): 1 skein each antique black #705 (A) and seaglass #708 (B)
- Size 4 (3.5mm) straight or circular needles or size needed to obtain gauge
- Stitch markers

1 SUPER FINE

Gauge
38 sts and 36 rows = 4 inches/10cm in Stripe pat (after blocking).

To save time, take time to check gauge.

Special Abbreviation
Right Twist (RT): Knit into 2nd st on LH needle but do not remove from needle, knit into first st, slipping both sts off needle.

Pattern Stitch
Stripe (multiple of 3 sts + 3)
Row 1 (WS): With B, p3, *sl 1 wyif, p2; rep from * across.
Row 2 (RS): With A, k1, *RT, sl 1 wyib; rep from * to last 2 sts, end k2.
Row 3: With A, *p2, sl 1 wyif; rep from * to last 3 sts, end p3.
Row 4: With B, k1, *sl 1 wyib, RT; rep from * to last 2 sts, end sl 1, k1.
Row 5: With B, p1, *sl 1 wyif, p2; rep from * to last 2 sts, end sl 1, p1.
Row 6: With A, *RT, sl 1 wyib; rep from * to last 3 sts, end RT, k1.

Rows 7–12: Rep Rows 1–6, reversing colors.

Rep Rows 1–12 for pat.

Pattern Notes
A chart is provided for those preferring to work stripe pattern from a chart.

Slip all stitches purlwise.

Border stitches are worked in same color as stripe pattern row.

Instructions
With A, cast on 4 sts for border, place marker, cast on 24 sts for stripe pat, place marker, cast on 4 sts border.

Work 4 rows in garter st.

Set-up row (RS): With B, k4 border sts, slip marker, *k2, sl 1 wyib; rep from * to 3 sts before marker, k3, slip marker, k4 border sts.

Beg with Row 1 of Stripe pat, work 4 border sts at each end in garter st and sts between markers in Stripe pat until piece measures 49½ inches or ½ inch less than desired length.

With A, work 4 rows in garter st.

Bind off loosely.

Soak and block or steam block to measurements. ●

STITCH & COLOR KEY
- □ K on RS, p on WS
- Ⅴ Sl 1 wyif
- ¥ Sl 1 wyib
- ⧄ RT
- ▨ A
- ▨ B

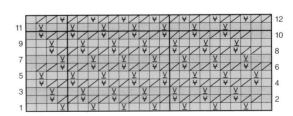

STRIPE CHART

On The Fringes

Fringe fanatics, you've found the right place. If you're looking for the tried and true basics, Chain Male delivers. For something cleverly different, Clarendon offers a new take on the traditional with woven eyelets, ending with a finale of fringe. If you're the daring sort, Stormy Weather will add a touch of bohemian flair to your winter attire.

Diamond in the Ruff

As the saying goes, "Diamonds are a girl's best friend." Adorn yourself in luxury when you wear this skinny scarf with tendrils of knit and purl diamonds

Design by Grace McEwen

Skill Level
◼◼◼◻ INTERMEDIATE

Finished Size
Approx 6 inches at widest point x 84 inches long, without fringe

Materials
- Malabrigo Merino Worsted (worsted weight; 100% merino wool; 210 yds/ 3.5oz per skein): 2 skeins blue graphite #508
- Size 8 (5mm) needles or size needed to obtain gauge

Gauge
20 sts and 25 rows = 4 inches/10cm in pat.
To save time, take time to check gauge.

Pattern Stitch
Diamond
Row 1: Yo, [k1, p2] 4 times, yo, k1—15 sts.
Row 2: Yo, [p1, k2] twice, p3, k2, p1, k2, yo, p1—17 sts.
Row 3: Yo, [k1, p2] twice, k5, p2, k1, p2, yo, k1—19 sts.
Row 4: Yo, [p1, k2] twice, p3, k1, p3, k2, p1, k2, yo, p1—21 sts.
Row 5: Yo, [k1, p2] twice, k3, p3, k3, p2, k1, p2, yo, k1—23 sts.
Row 6: Yo, [p1, k2] twice, p3, k5, p3, k2, p1, k2, yo, p1—25 sts.
Row 7: Yo, [k1, p2] twice, k3, p7, k3, p2, k1, p2, yo, k1—27 sts.
Row 8: Yo, [p1, k2] twice, p3, k9, p3, k2, p1, k2, yo, p1—29 sts.
Row 9: Yo, k1, p2tog, k1, p2, k3, p11, k3, p2, k1, k2tog, yo, k1.

Row 10: Yo, p3tog, k1, p1, k2, p3, k9, p3, k2, p1, k3tog, yo, k1—27 sts.
Row 11: Yo, p3tog, p1, k1, p2, k3, p7, k3, p2, k1, k3tog, yo, p1—25 sts.
Row 12: Yo, p3tog, k1, p1, k2, p3, k5, p3, k2, p1, k3tog, yo, k1—23 sts.
Row 13: Yo, p3tog, p1, k1, p2, k3, p3, k3, p2, k1, k3tog, yo, p1—21 sts.
Row 14: Yo, p3tog, k1, p1, k2, p3, k1, p3, k2, p1, k3tog, yo, k1—19 sts.
Row 15: Yo, p3tog, p1, k1, p2, k5, p2, k1, k3tog, yo, p1—17 sts.
Row 16: Yo, p3tog, k1, p1, k2, p3, k2, p1, k3tog, yo, k1—15 sts.
Row 17: Yo, p3tog, p1, k1, p2, k1, p2, k1, k3tog, yo, p1—13 sts.
Row 18: K1, [p2, k1] 4 times.

Rep Rows 1–18 for pat.

Pattern Note
Since scarf is reversible, no right or wrong side is indicated.

Scarf
Cast on 13 sts.

Work Rows 1–18 of Diamond pat until scarf measures 84 inches or desired length.

Bind off loosely.

For fringe: Cut 20 (16-inch) lengths of yarn. For each knot, fold 10 lengths in half. Take folded-loop section through bottom point of one end of scarf. Loop the ends through and pull tightly to secure. Trim ends even.

Block to measurements. ●

Chain Male

Working with one color at a time and simple slipped stitches, this manly scarf looks intricate but is easy to create.

Design by Allison Harding

Skill Level
■■□□ EASY

Finished Size
Approx 6½ inches wide x 64 inches long without fringe, after blocking

Materials
- Berroco Comfort DK (DK weight; 50% super fine nylon/50% super fine acrylic; 178 yds/50g per ball): 2 balls hummus #2720 (MC), 1 ball each bittersweet #2741 (A) and navy blue #2763 (B)
- Size 4 (3.5mm) straight or 32-inch (or longer) circular needle or size needed to obtain gauge

3 LIGHT

Gauge
20 sts and 40 rows = 4 inches/10cm in St st.
To save time, take time to check gauge.

Pattern Stitch
Chains (multiple of 8 sts + 6)
Row 1 (RS): With MC, knit across.
Row 2: Purl across. Drop MC, do not cut yarn.
Row 3: With A, knit across.
Row 4: Knit across. Drop A, do not cut yarn.
Row 5: With MC, k6, *sl 2 wyib, k6; rep from * across.
Row 6: P6, *sl 2 wyif, p6; rep from * across. Drop MC, do not cut yarn.
Row 7: With A, k6, *sl 2 wyib, k6; rep from * across.
Row 8: Knit across. Cut A.
Rows 9 and 10: Rep Rows 1 and 2.
Row 11: With B, knit across.
Row 12: Knit across. Drop B, do not cut yarn.
Row 13: With MC, k2, *sl 2 wyib, k6; rep from * across.
Row 14: P2, *sl 2 wyif, p6; rep from * across. Drop MC, do not cut yarn.
Row 15: With B, k2, *sl 2 wyib, k6; rep from * across.
Row 16: Knit across. Cut B.

Rep Rows 1–16 for pat.

Special Technique
Sewn Bind-Off: Thread tapestry needle with yarn approx 4 times the length of edge to be bound off. With sts on knitting needle in left hand, *pull tapestry needle through 2 front loops as if to purl, then back through the first st as if to knit; drop first st off needle; rep from * to the end.

Pattern Notes
This scarf is worked lengthwise using only one color per row. Main color is carried along the edge and used as needed. Contrast colors A and B are cut and reattached as indicated. The scarf length may be adjusted by multiples of 8 stitches.

When adding or finishing off contrast-color yarns at beginning and end of row, leave a long tail to incorporate into fringe rather than weaving it into the scarf.

For a long tail cast-on requiring a large number of stitches, use a strand of the same color from two different balls of yarn, one for the tail and the other to place the stitches on the needle. The tail will never be too short no matter how many stitches you cast on.

For best results, use a long tail cast-on with a sewn bind off.

Scarf
With MC, cast on 286 sts. Knit 1 row.

Work [Rows 1–16 of Chain pat] 4 times or until 1 inch less than desired width.

Rep Rows 1–10.

With MC, purl 1 row.

With WS facing, bind off using sewn bind-off.

Fringe
Cut 80 strands MC, 40 strands of A and 32 strands B, 11 inches long or twice desired finished length plus 1 inch. Using 4 strands for each knot and following color sequence of pat, place knot in each MC stripe and chain. Trim ends even.

Steam block. ●

Stormy Weather

Lengthwise stripes knit with sport weight yarn on large needles create a fabric that can be wrapped around the neck once, or several times for maximum warmth. The braided fringe adds drama without adding weight or bulk.

Design by Ann Weaver

. . . .

Skill Level
◼◻◻◻ BEGINNER

Finished Size
Approx 7 inches wide x 85 inches long, without fringe

Materials
- Brown Sheep Top of the Lamb (sport weight; 100% wool; 350 yds/ 100g per skein): 1 skein each grey heather #113 (MC) and charcoal heather #114 (CC)
- Size 11 (8mm) 40-inch circular needle or size needed to obtain gauge
- Size H/8 (5mm) crochet hook for attaching fringe

2 FINE

Gauge
12 sts and 20 rows = 4 inches/10cm in St st.
To save time, take time to check gauge.

Pattern Note
As scarf is reversible, there is no right or wrong side indicated. When adding fringe knots, pick one side of the scarf to treat as right side and attach fringe consistently.

Scarf
With MC, cast on 240 sts. Knit 1 row. Change to CC.

Row 1: Purl across.

Row 2: Knit across.

Rows 3 and 4: Rep Rows 1 and 2. Cut MC.

Row 5: With CC, k1, *wyif, insert tip of LH needle from top down into MC, purl st 4 rows below the next st on needle, place this loop on LH needle and purl tog with the next st; rep from * to last st, end k1.

Rows 6–11: With MC, rep [Rows 1 and 2] 3 times.

Row 12: Purl across.

Row 13: With CC, knit across.

Rows 14 and 15: Rep Rows 1 and 2.

Row 16: Purl across.

Row 17: Rep Row 5.

Rows 18–23: With MC [rep Rows 1 and 2] 3 times.

Row 24: Purl across.

Rep Rows 1–24, then rep Rows 1–5.

With MC, purl 1 row. Bind off loosely.

Finishing
Block to measurements.

Braided fringe
Cut 48 (28-inch) lengths of CC and 42 (28-inch) lengths of MC.

Fringe knots are attached at ends of CC cords at both ends of the scarf. For first, 3rd, and 5th cords, use 6 lengths of CC and 3 lengths of MC for each knot; for 2nd and 4th cords, use 3 lengths of CC and 6 lengths of MC.

To make fringe knot braid: Hold 9 lengths of yarn tog and fold in half. Insert crochet hook from back to front through scarf and folded yarn. Pull yarn through scarf, drawing ends of fringe through loop, and pull tight. Braid fringe by dividing yarn in each knot into 3 groups, each strand composed of 6 strands of MC or CC yarn. Braid fringe until approximately 2 inches rem unbraided. Tie braid ends and pull tight. Trim fringe ends even. ●

Clarendon

Inspired by a classic tweed jacket, this scarf creates a tailored look that's soft and easy to wear.

Design by Tracy Wells

Skill Level

■■□□ EASY

Finished Size
Approx 6 wide x 45 inches long, without fringe

Materials
- Knit One, Crochet Too 2nd Time Cotton (worsted weight; 75% recycled cotton/25% acrylic; 180 yds/100g per skein): 2 skeins ochre #485 (MC)
- Knit One, Crochet Too Linus (worsted weight; 47% wool/30% acrylic/23% alpaca; 98 yds/ 50g per ball): 1 ball cherry #257 (CC)
- Size 7 (4.5mm) needles or size needed to obtain gauge
- Stitch marker

Gauge
20 sts and 24 rows = 4 inches/10cm in pat.
To save time, take time to check gauge.

Pattern Note
As scarf is reversible it is helpful to place a marker on Row 1 to keep track of rows.

Scarf
With MC, cast on 30 sts.

Knit 3 rows.

Row 1: K3, [k2tog] 12 times, k3—18 sts.

Row 2: K3, [yo, k1] 12 times, k3—30 sts.

Rows 3 and 4: Knit across.

Rep Rows 1–4 until scarf measures 44 inches or 1 inch less than desired length.

Knit 3 rows.

Bind off loosely.

Basket weave
Cut 48 strands of CC approx 16 inches longer than length of scarf.

Thread tapestry needle with 4 strands of CC.

Starting at one narrow end of the scarf, weave yarn through the holes created by yo's, leaving an even amount of yarn at each end for the fringe and smoothing to keep scarf flat.

Referring to photo, continue weaving yarn through yo's in a basket weave pat until all 12 holes across have been filled with CC yarn.

Fringe
Tie 2 sets of 4 CC yarn strands tog, creating 6 knots of fringe across each end. If desired, use additional CC yarn to create short fringes at each corner of the scarf. Trim to desired length. ●

Something Sassy

You'll find just the right assortment of adornments in this delightful collection of scarflettes, capelettes and neck warmers. Find a little piece of heaven wearing Ethereal Dream, made in the softest kid mohair. With drop-stitch styling, and wearing options abound, Infinity & Beyond is sure to satisfy.

Infinity & Beyond

This chunky cowl knits up in a flash and gives the wearer endless styling options due to the clever addition of large buttons and dropped stitches. Just twist, fold or roll the scarf into your desired look, pop one or both of the buttons through a dropped stitch, and you're ready to hit the catwalk!

Design by Sarah Wilson

Skill Level
■□□□ BEGINNER

Finished Size
Circumference: 26 inches
Width: 8 inches

Materials
- Plymouth Baby Alpaca Grande (bulky weight; 100% alpaca; 110 yards/ 100g per skein): 1 skein brown #302
- Size 11 (8mm) 16-inch circular needle or size needed to obtain gauge
- Stitch marker
- 2 (2½-inch) buttons
- Sewing needle and matching thread

Gauge
11 sts and 21 rows = 4 inches/10cm in garter st.
To save time, take time to check gauge.

Scarf
Cast on 48 sts. Place marker for beg of rnd and join, being careful not to twist sts.

Work in garter st (knit 1 rnd, purl 1 rnd) until piece measures 8 inches from cast-on edge.

Bind off as follows: *Bind off 4 sts, draw up a large loop from the last bound-off st and pass the entire skein of yarn through loop, drawing close to secure the st; drop next st off needle and allow it to unravel down to the cast-on row; loosely carry yarn across dropped st; rep from * around.

Finishing
Stretch gently to ensure all dropped sts have unraveled.

Sew on buttons. Twist, fold or roll scarf as desired, using drop st area for buttonholes. ●

Ethereal Dream

This dainty, all-garter–stitch scarf provides a great way for beginners to practice simple shaping. It is also a quick knit for more advanced knitters needing a last-minute gift.

Design by Michelle Heaney

· ·

Skill Level
◼☐☐☐ BEGINNER

Finished Size
Approx 4½ inches wide across center section x 30 inches long

Materials
- Rowan Kidsilk Haze (lace weight; 70% super kid mohair/30% silk; 229 yds/25g per ball); 1 ball pearl #590
- Size 5 (3.75mm) needles or size needed to obtain gauge

Gauge
24 sts and 36 rows = 4 inches/ 10 cm in garter st. To save time, take time to check gauge.

Special Abbreviations
Increase (inc): Inc 1 by knitting in front and back of next st.

Knit in front, back and front (kfbf): Inc 2 sts by knitting in front, back and then front again of next st.

Pattern Note
As this scarflette is reversible, it is helpful to place a marker on Row 1 to indicate odd-numbered rows.

Scarflette
Cast on 1 st.

Double-opening end
Increase rows

Row 1: Kfbf—3 sts.

Rows 2–4: Knit across.

Row 5: [Inc] twice, k1—5 sts.

Rows 6–8: Knit across.

Row 9: Inc, k2, inc, k1—7 sts.

Rows 10–13: Knit across.

Row 14: Inc, k4, inc, k1—9 sts.

Rows 15–18: Knit across.

Row 19: Inc, k6, inc, k1—11 sts.

Rows 20–24: Knit across.

Row 25: Inc, k8, inc, k1—13 sts.

Rows 26–30: Knit across.

Row 31: Inc, k10, inc, k1—15 sts.

Rows 32–37: Knit across.

Row 38: Inc, k12, inc, k1—17 sts.

Rows 39–44: Knit across.

Row 45: Inc, k14, inc, k1—19 sts.

Rows 46–52: Knit across.

Row 53: Inc, k16, inc, k1—21 sts.

Rows 54–60: Knit across.

Row 61: Inc, k18, inc, k1—23 sts.

Rows 62–69: Knit across.

Row 70: Inc, k20, inc, k1—25 sts.

Rows 71–78: Knit across.

Row 79: Inc, k22, inc, k1—27 sts.

Row 80: K11, bind off 5, k11 (includes st on needle after bind-off)—22 sts.

Row 81: K11, cast on 5 sts, k11—27 sts.

Rows 82–87: Knit across.

Row 88: K11, bind off 5 sts, k11—22 sts.

Row 89: K11, cast on 5 sts, k11—27 sts.

Center

Knit even until scarflette from Row 89 measures 10½ inches.

Single-opening end
Decrease rows

Row 1: K11, bind off 5 sts, k11 (includes st on needle after bind off)—22 sts.

Row 2: K11, cast on 5 sts, k11—27 sts.

Row 3: Knit across.

Row 4: Ssk, k23, k2tog—25 sts.

Rows 5–12: Knit across.

Row 13: Ssk, k21, k2tog—23 sts.

Rows 14–21: Knit across.

Row 22: Ssk, k19, k2tog—21 sts.

Rows 23–29: Knit across.

Row 30: Ssk, k17, k2tog—19 sts.

Rows 31–37: Knit across.

Row 38: Ssk, k15, k2tog—17 sts.

Rows 39–44: Knit across.

Row 45: Ssk, k13, k2tog—15 sts.

Rows 46–51: Knit across.

Row 52: Ssk, k11, k2tog—13 sts.

Rows 53–57: Knit across.

Row 58: Ssk, k9, k2tog—11 sts.

Rows 59–63: Knit across.

Row 64: Ssk, k7, k2tog—9 sts.

Rows 65–68: Knit across.

Row 69: Ssk, k5, k2tog—7 sts.

Rows 70–73: Knit across.

Row 74: Ssk, k3, k2tog—5 sts.

Rows 75–77: Knit across.

Row 78: Ssk, k1, k2tog—3 sts.

Row 79: K3tog. Finish off.

To wear: Slide double-opening end from back to front through single opening, and then slide single-opening end through double opening belt loop. ●

Plissados

It's all about the ruffles—fun, flirty and flattering.

Design by Jean Clement

Skill Level

 EASY

Finished Size
Approx 12 inches x 31 inches

Materials
- Malabrigo Sock (fingering weight; 100% superwash merino wool; 440 yds/100g per skein): 1 skein lettuce #37
- Size 7 (4.5mm) 40-inch circular needle or size needed to obtain gauge

SUPER FINE 1

Gauge
23 sts and 24 rows = 4 inches/10cm in St st.
To save time, take time to check gauge.

Pattern Notes
Sample project uses the entire skein of yarn. If working to a gauge different from gauge given, purchase an additional skein to ensure you have sufficient yarn to complete the project.

Circular needle is used to accommodate large number of stitches. Do not join, work back and forth in rows.

To obtain the ruffling shape of this scarf, multiple increases are made on every right-side row. As number of stitches quickly becomes rather large, the stitch count is only given every 18 rows, with the last count after the last 12 rows. While there are quite a few stitches when the bind-off row is reached, it is all easy knitting.

Scarf
Using long tail cast-on and leaving a 12-inch tail, cast on 19 sts. Knit 1 row using both working yarn and cast-on tail.

Row 1 (RS): Sl 1, k2, [yo, k1, yo, k3] 4 times (8 sts inc).

Row 2 and all WS rows: Purl across.

Row 3: Sl 1, k2, *yo, k3, yo, k3; rep from * across.

Row 5: Sl 1, k2, *yo, k5, yo, k3; rep from * across.

Row 7: Sl 1, k2, *yo, k7, yo, k3; rep from * across.

Row 9: Sl 1, k2, *yo, k9, yo, k3; rep from * across.

Row 11: Sl 1, k2, *yo, k11, yo, k3; rep from * across.

Row 13: Sl 1, k2, *yo, k13, yo, k3; rep from * across.

Row 15: Sl 1, k2, *yo, k15, yo, k3; rep from * across.

Row 17: Sl 1, k2, *yo, k17, yo, k3; rep from * across—91 sts.

Row 19: Sl 1, k2, *yo, k9, yo, k1, yo, k9, yo, k3; rep from * across (16 sts inc).

Row 21: Sl 1, k2, *yo, k10, yo, k3, yo, k10, yo, k3; rep from * across.

Row 23: Sl 1, k2, *yo, k11, yo, k5, yo, k11, yo, k3; rep from * across.

Row 25: Sl 1, k2, *yo, k12, yo, k7, yo, k12, yo, k3; rep from * across.

Row 27: Sl 1, k2, *yo, k13, yo, k9, yo, k13, yo, k3; rep from * across.

Row 29: Sl 1, k2, *yo, k14, yo, k11, yo, k14, yo, k3; rep from * across.

Row 31: Sl 1, k2, *yo, k15, yo, k13, yo, k15, yo, k3; rep from * across.

Row 33: Sl 1, k2, *yo, k16, yo, k15, yo, k16, yo, k3; rep from * across.

Row 35: Sl 1, k2, *yo, k17, yo, k17, yo, k17, yo, k3; rep from * across—235 sts.

Row 37: Sl 1, k2, *yo, k18, yo, k9, yo, k1, yo, k9, yo, k18, yo, k3; rep from * across (24 sts inc).

Row 39: Sl 1, k2, *yo, k19, yo, k10, yo, k3, yo, k10, yo, k19, yo, k3; rep from * across.

Row 41: Sl 1, k2, *yo, k20, yo, k11, yo, k5, yo, k11, yo, k20, yo, k3; rep from * across.

Row 43: Sl 1, k2, *yo, k21, yo, k12, yo, k7, yo, k12, yo, k21, yo, k3; rep from * across.

Row 45: Sl 1, k2, *yo, k22, yo, k13, yo, k9, yo, k13, yo, k22, yo, k3; rep from * across.

Row 47: Sl 1, k2, *yo, k23, yo, k14, yo, k11, yo, k14, yo, k23, yo, k3; rep from * across.

Row 49: Sl 1, k2, *yo, k24, yo, k15, yo, k13, yo, k15, yo, k24, yo, k3; rep from * across.

Row 51: Sl 1, k2, *yo, k25, yo, k16, yo, k15, yo, k16, yo, k25, yo, k3; rep from * across.

Row 53: Sl 1, k2, *yo, k26, yo, k17, yo, k17, yo, k17, yo, k26, yo, k3; rep from * across—451 sts.

Row 55: Sl 1, k2, *yo, k27, yo, k18, yo, k9, yo, k1, yo, k9, yo, k18, yo, k27, yo, k3; rep from * across (32 sts inc).

Row 57: Sl 1, k2, *yo, k28, yo, k19, yo, k10, yo, k3, yo, k10, yo, k19, yo, k28, yo, k3; rep from * across.

Row 59: Sl 1, k2, *yo, k29, yo, k20, yo, k11, yo, k5, yo, k11, yo, k20, yo, k29, yo, k3; rep from * across.

Row 61: Sl 1, k2, *yo, k30, yo, k21, yo, k12, yo, k7, yo, k12, yo, k21, yo, k30, yo, k3; rep from * across.

Row 63: Sl 1, k2, *yo, k31, yo, k22, yo, k13, yo, k9, yo, k13, yo, k22, yo, k31, yo, k3; rep from * across.

Row 65: Sl 1, k2, *yo, k32, yo, k23, yo, k14, yo, k11, yo, k14, yo, k23, yo, k32, yo, k3; rep from * across—643 sts.

Row 66: Purl across.

Border

Row 1 (RS): Sl 1, k2, *[yo, k3] 26 times, yo, k1, [yo, k3] 27 times; rep from * across—859 sts.

Row 2: Purl across.

Row 3: Sl 1, *k1, yo; rep from * to last 2 sts, k2—1,715 sts.

Bind off as follows: *P2tog, 1 st on RH needle, slip st back to LH needle; rep from * across. Fasten off.

Finishing
Block gently. ●

This Way & That

If your interest is meandering ribs, The Long & Winding Road will take you there. If cables are your forte, you may find Pineapple Hearts to be just the challenge you've up for. Or perhaps, you'd like to mix it up with something unexpected; the Chunky Drop Stitch Cable Warmer may suit your fancy.

Meanderlust

This neck warmer makes full use of the unique qualities of thick and thin yarn with a straightforward cable pattern and lace edging.

Design by Linda Wilgus

Skill Level
■■■☐ INTERMEDIATE

Finished Size
Approx 6½ x 22 inches

Materials
- Cascade Yarns Jewel (chunky weight; 100% wool; 142 yds/100g per skein): 1 skein tan #9263
- Size 9 (5.5mm) needles or size needed to obtain gauge
- 2 (1½-inch) buttons
- Cable needle

5 BULKY

Gauge
23 sts and 21 rows = 4 inches/10cm in Honeycomb Cable pat.
To save time, take time to check gauge.

Special Abbreviations
Cable over 4 front (C4F): Slip next 2 sts on cn and hold to front, k2, k2 from cn.

Cable over 4 back (C4B): Slip next 2 sts on cn and hold to back, k2, k2 from cn.

Pattern Stitches
Note: Charts are provided for those preferring to work pattern sts from a chart.

Honeycomb Cable
Row 1 (RS): K2, p2, [C4B, C4F] twice, p2, k2.
Rows 2, 4 and 6: P2, k2, purl to last 4 sts, k2, p2.
Rows 3 and 7: K2, p2, knit to last 4 sts, p2, k2.
Row 5: K2, p2, [C4F, C4B] twice, p2, k2.
Row 8: P2, k2, purl to last 4 sts, k2, p2.

Rep Rows 1–8 for pat.

Lace Edging
Row 1 (RS): K2, yo, k2tog, yo, k2—7 sts.
Row 2: K2, [yo, k1] twice, yo, k2tog, k1—9 sts.
Row 3: K2, yo, k2tog, yo, k3, yo, k2—11 sts.
Row 4: K2, yo, k5, yo, k1, yo, k2tog, k1—13 sts.
Row 5: K2, yo, k2tog, yo, ssk, k3, k2tog, yo, k2.
Row 6: K3, yo, ssk, k1, k2tog, yo, k2, yo, k2tog, k1.
Row 7: K2, yo, k2tog, k2, yo, sk2p, yo, k4.
Row 8: Bind off 7 sts, k3 (including st on needle after bind-off), yo, k2tog, k1—6 sts.

Rep Rows 1–8 for pat.

Special Technique
Cable cast-on: Place needle with last st worked in LH. Knit st but do not drop st from needle. Insert LH needle in the front loop of new st and transfer to LH needle. *Insert RH needle between new st and old st and knit a st. Transfer new st to LH needle as before. Rep from * for desired number of sts.

Scarf
Cast on 24 sts.

Set-up row (WS): P2, k2, purl to last 4 sts, k2, p2.

Work [Rows 1–8 of Honeycomb Cable pat] 14 times. Scarf should measure approx 19 inches.

Buttonholes
Row 1 (RS): K2, p2, [C4B, C4F] twice, p2, k2.

Row 2: P2, k2, p2, bind off the next 4 sts, p4 (including st on needle after bind-off), bind off the next 4 sts, p2 (including st on needle after bind-off), k2, p2—16 sts.

Row 3: K2, p2, k2, cast on 4 sts using cable cast-on, k4, cast on 4 sts using cable cast-on, k2, p2, k2—20 sts.

Rows 4 and 6: P2, k2, purl to last 4 sts, k2, p2.

Row 5: K2, p2, [C4F, C4B] twice, p2, k2.

Row 7: K2, p2, knit to last 4 sts, p2, k2.

Row 8: P2, k2, purl to last 4 sts, k2, p2.

Work Rows 1–8 of Honeycomb Cable pat until work measures 22 inches.

Bind off all sts.

Edging
Cast on 6 sts.

Knit 1 row.

Work Rows 1–8 of Lace Edging pat until edging measures 22 inches, ending with Row 8 of pat. Bind off all sts.

Finishing
Place scarf flat with RS facing and buttonholes to right. Place lace edging flat along bottom long edge and sew in place. Attach buttons as desired, opposite buttonholes.

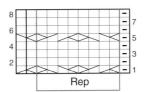

HONEYCOMB CABLE CHART

STITCH KEY	
☐	K on RS, p on WS
–	P on RS, k on WS
⤬	C4F
⤬	C4B

LACE EDGING CHART

STITCH KEY	
☐	K on RS, p on WS
–	P on RS, k on WS
O	Yo
⁄	K2tog
\	Ssk
⋀	Sk2p
∩	Bind off
■	No st

Pineapple Hearts

This intriguing design with crossing cables offers a variety of wearing options to suit your mood.

Design by Dawn Brocco

. . . .

Skill Level
■■■■□ EXPERIENCED

Finished Size
Approx 6½ inches wide x 39½ inches long

Materials
- Cascade Yarns Cloud 9 (worsted weight; 50% wool/50% angora; 109 yds/ 50g per ball): 4 balls soft rose #143
- Size 10½ (6.5mm) needles or size needed to obtain gauge
- Cable needle

4 MEDIUM

Gauge
12 sts and 17 rows = 4 inches/10cm in St st with 2 strands of yarn held tog.
14 sts and 17 rows = 4 inches in K6, P1 Rib with 2 strands of yarn held tog.
To save time, take time to check gauge.

Special Abbreviations
Make 1 to Left (M1L): Knit next st, then insert tip of LH needle into the left side of st 2 rows below st just made on RH needle and knit it.

Make 1 to Right (M1R): Insert tip of RH needle into right side of st below st on LH needle and knit into it, then knit next st.

Make 3 (M3): At beg of WS rows, in first st, work [k1, p1] twice. At end of WS rows, in last st, work [p1, k1] twice.

Decrease 3 stitches (Dec 3): Ssk next 2 sts, k2tog in rem 2 sts, pass ssk over k2tog.

3 over 3 Right Purl Cross (3/3RPC): Slip next 3 sts to cn and hold in back, k3, p3 from cn.

3 over 3 Left Purl Cross (3/3LPC): Slip next 3 sts to cn and hold in front, p3, k3 from cn.

3 over 2 Right Purl Cross (3/2RPC): Slip next 2 sts to cn and hold in back, k3, p2 from cn.

3 over 2 Left Purl Cross (3/2LPC): Slip next 3 sts to cn and hold in front, p2, k3 from cn.

3 over 1 Right Purl Cross (3/1RPC): Slip next st to cn and hold in back, k3, p1 from cn.

3 over 1 Left Purl Cross (3/1LPC): Slip next 3 sts to cn and hold in front, p1, k3 from cn.

3 over 3 Right Cross (3/3RC): Slip next 3 sts to cn and hold in back, k3, k3 from cn.

3 over 3 Left Cross (3/3LC): Slip next 3 sts to cn and hold in front, k3, k3 from cn.

Pattern Notes
Yarn is worked double throughout.

Shaped cables are made by working each side separately, then joining, and then separating again for open center, increasing and decreasing to shape the cables.

A chart is provided for those preferring to work pattern from a chart; however, if you choose to follow the chart, refer to the written instructions, if necessary, for clarification. On the chart odd-numbered rows are wrong-side rows and are worked from left to right; even-numbered rows are right-side rows and are worked from right to left.

An edge stitch worked in stockinette stitch at each side is included in the written instructions but is not shown on the chart.

Scarf

Cable edge
With 2 strands of yarn held tog, cast on 18 left-side sts. With another 2 strands of yarn held tog, cast on 18 right-side sts.

Follow chart, beg with Row 1, a WS row, or written instructions below.

Row 1 (WS): P1 (edge st), k1, [p3, k3] twice, p3, M1L on first side; M1R, [p3, k3] twice, p3, k1, p1 (edge st) on 2nd side—38 sts.

Row 2 (RS): K1 (edge st), p1, [k3, p3] twice, 3/1LPC, p1; p1, 3/1RPC, [k3, p3] twice, p1, k1 (edge st).

Row 3: P1, k1, p3, k3, p3, k4, p3, M1L; M1R, p3, k4, p3, k3, p3, k1, p1—40 sts.

Row 4 (joining row): K1, p1, k3, p3, 3/2LPC, p2, 3/1LPC, p1, with same yarn, p1, 3/1RPC, p2, 3/2RPC, p3, k3, p1, k1. Cut extra yarn.

Row 5: P1, k1, p3, k5, p3, k3, p3, k2, p3, k3, p3, k5, p3, k1, p1.

Row 6: K1, p1, 3/3LPC, p2, 3/2LPC, p1, 3/1LPC, 3/1RPC, p1, 3/2RPC, p2, 3/3RPC, p1, k1.

Row 7: P1, Dec 3, p3, k4, p3, k2, p6, k2, p3, k4, p3, Dec 3, p1–34 sts.

Row 8: K1, p1, 3/3LPC, p1, 3/2LPC, 3/3RC, 3/2RPC, p1, 3/3RPC, p1, k1.

Row 9: P1, Dec 3, p3, k3, p12, k3, p3, Dec 3, p1—28 sts.

Row 10: K1, p1, 3/3LPC, [3/3LC] twice, 3/3RPC, p1, k1.

Row 11: P1, Dec 3, p18, Dec 3, p1—22 sts.

Row 12: K1, p1, [3/3RC] 3 times, p1, k1.

Row 13: P1, M3, p18, M3, p1—28 sts.

Row 14: K1, p1, 3/3RPC, [3/3LC] twice, 3/3LPC, p1, k1.

Row 15: P1, M3, p3, k3, p12, k3, p3, M3, p1—34 sts.

Row 16: K1, p1, 3/3RPC, p1, 3/2RPC, 3/3RC, 3/2LPC, p1, 3/3LPC, p1, k1.

Row 17: P1, k1, M3, p3, k4, p3, k2, p6, k2, p3, k4, p3, M3, p1—40 sts.

Row 18: K1, p1, 3/3RPC, p2, 3/2RPC, p1, 3/1RPC, 3/1LPC, p1, 3/2LPC, p2, 3/3LPC, p1, k1.

Row 19: P1, k1, p3, k5, p3, k3, p3, k2, p3, k3, p3, k5, p3, k1, p1.

Row 20 (separating row): K1, p1, k3, p3, 3/2RPC, p2, 3/1RPC, p1; with another 2 strands, p1, 3/1LPC, p2, 3/2LPC, p3, k3, p1, k1.

Row 21: P1, k1, p3, k3, p3, k4, p3, k2tog, ssk, p3, k4, p3, k3, p3, k1, p1—38 sts.

Row 22: K1, p1, [k3, p3] twice, 3/1RPC, p1; p1, 3/1LPC, [k3, p3] twice, p1, k1.

Row 23: P1, k1, [p3, k3] twice, p3, k2tog; ssk, [p3, k3] twice, p3, k1, p1—36 sts.

Row 24: K1, p1, [k3, p3] twice, k3, p1; p1, [k3, p3] twice, k3, p1, k1.

Rows 25-36: Rep Rows 1–12.

Center ribbing

Row 37 (set-up row): P1, k1, *p5, [p1, k1] in next st; rep from * once more, p6, k1, p1—24 sts.

Row 38: K1, p1, [k6, p1] twice, k6, p1, k1.

Row 39: P1, k1, [p6, k1] twice, p6, k1, p1.

Rep Rows 38 and 39 until ribbing section measures approx 18 inches (28 inches from cast-on edge) ending with a WS row.

Cable edge with buttonhole

Next row (RS): K1, p1, k6, [k2tog, k5] twice, p1, k1—22 sts.

Next row (WS): P1, k1, p18, k1, p1.

Rep Rows 12–24 of chart, then rep Rows 1–22. Bind off in pat, following Row 23.

Finishing

Block to measurements. ●

STITCH KEY	
☐	K on RS, p on WS
−	P on RS, k on WS
▨	No st
╱	Ssk (on RS)
╲	K2tog (on WS)
⊻	M3
▲	Dec 3
M	M1L or M1R
╲╱	3/1 LPC
╱╲	3/1 RPC
╲╱	3/3 LC
╱╲	3/3 RC
╱╲	3/3 RPC
╲╱	3/3 LPC
╱╲	3/2 RPC
╲╱	3/2 LPC

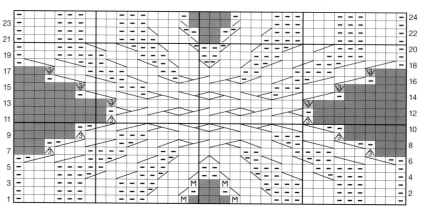

CABLE CHART

Note: 1 edge st on each side is not included on chart.

The Long & Winding Road

This scarf combines a cosmopolitan style with simple construction, using increases and decreases to achieve a swirling effect.

Design by Susan Dittrich

Skill Level

■■■□ INTERMEDIATE

Finished Size
Approx 6 inches wide x 80 inches long

Materials
- Katia Peru (chunky weight; 40% wool/ 40% acrylic/20% alpaca 116 yds/ 100g per ball): 3 balls slate blue #18
- Size 10 (6mm) needles or size needed to obtain gauge

5 BULKY

Gauge
14 sts and 19 rows = 4 inches/10cm in Garter Swirl pat.
To save time, take time to check gauge.

Special Abbreviations
Make 1 (M1): Insert LH needle from front to back under horizontal strand between last st worked and next st on LH needle, k1-tbl.

Make 1 purlwise (M1-p): Insert LH needle from front to back under horizontal strand between last st worked and next st on LH needle, p1-tbl.

Pattern Stitch
Garter Swirl (panel of 22 sts)
Row 1 and all WS rows: Purl across.
Row 2 (RS): *P2, k2; rep from * to last 2 sts, p2.
Rows 4 and 6: Rep Row 2.
Row 8: P2, M1, [k2, p2] twice, k1, ssk, p1, [k2, p2] twice.
Row 10: P2, k1, M1, [k2, p2] twice, k1, ssk, [k2, p2] twice.

Row 12: P2, k2, M1-p, [k2, p2] twice, k1, ssk, k1, p2, k2, p2.
Row 14: P2, k2, p1, M1-p, [k2, p2] twice, k1, ssk, p2, k2, p2.
Row 16: P2, k2, p2, M1, [k2, p2] twice, k1, ssk, p1, k2, p2.
Row 18: P2, k2, p2, k1, M1, [k2, p2] twice, k1, ssk, k2, p2.
Row 20: [P2, k2] twice, M1-p, [k2, p2] twice, k1, ssk, k1, p2.
Row 22: [P2, k2] twice, p1, M1-p, [k2, p2] twice, k1, ssk, p2.
Rows 24, 26 and 28: Rep Row 2.
Row 30: P2, k2, p2, M1, k2, p2, k1, ssk, p1, [k2, p2] twice.
Row 32: P2, k2, p2, k1, M1, k2, p2, k1, ssk, [k2, p2] twice.
Row 34: [P2, k2] twice, M1-p, k2, p2, k1, ssk, k1, p2, k2, p2.
Row 36: [P2, k2] twice, p1, M1-p, k2, p2, k1, ssk, p2, k2, p2.

Rep Rows 1–36 for pat.

Pattern Note
A chart is provided for those preferring to work pattern stitch from a chart.

Scarf
Cast on 22 sts.

Work [Rows 1–36 of Garter Swirl pat] 10 times, then rep Rows 1–29.

Bind off loosely. Block to measurements. ●

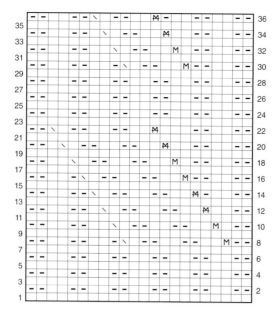

GARTER SWIRL CHART

Chunky Drop Stitch Cable Warmer

Intentionally dropped stitches make cables pop and add interest to this cozy, versatile neck warmer.

Design by Betsy Farquhar

. . . .

Skill Level

■ ■ ■ □ INTERMEDIATE

Finished Size
Approx 11½ inches wide (sewn) x 7¼ inches tall

Materials
- Shibui Knits Highland Wool Alpaca (chunky weight; 80% wool/20% alpaca; 8¾ oz/246 yds/250g per skein): 1 skein wasabi #7495 (*Note: About 5 oz is needed for project.*)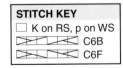
- Size 10½ (6.5mm) needles (needles should be 14 inches long or longer) or size needed to obtain gauge
- Cable needle

Gauge
18 sts and 14 rows = 4 inches/10cm in cable panel. To save time, take time to check your gauge.

Special Abbreviations
Cable 6 Back (C6B): Sl 3 sts onto cn and hold in back, k3, k3 from cn.

Cable 6 Front (C6F): Sl 3 sts onto cn and hold in front, k3, k3 from cn.

Pattern Stitch
Smocked Cable (multiple of 24 sts)
Row 1 (RS): [C6B] 4 times.
Row 2: Purl across.
Row 3: Knit across.
Row 4: Purl across.
Row 5: K3, [C6F] 3 times, k3.
Row 6: Purl across.
Row 7: Knit across.
Row 8: Purl across.

Rep Rows 1–8 for pat.

Scarf
Cast on 101 sts. Purl 1 row.

Set up pat
Row 1 (RS): [Work Row 1 of Smocked Cable pat over 24 sts, k1] 4 times, k1 (edge st).

Row 2: P1 (edge st), [p1, work Row 2 of Smocked Cable pat] 4 times.

Continue to work in established Smocked Cable pat separated by 1 st in St st until 6 rep of pat are complete.

Purl 1 row.

Bind-off pat
Bind off working Row 1 of Smocked Cable pat, dropping every 25th st (st between cables) off needle. Use very loose st to bind off between cables where st was dropped.

Pull st to drop to cast-on edge.

Finishing
With RS facing, bring ends of rows tog to form a tube with edges overlapping, placing edge st under first cable panel. Sew edges tog. ●

STITCH KEY
□ K on RS, p on WS
C6B
C6F

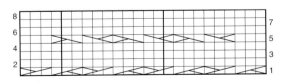

SMOCKED CABLE PANEL

General Information

Abbreviations & Symbols

[ ] work instructions within brackets as many times as directed

( ) work instructions within parentheses in the place directed

** repeat instructions following the asterisks as directed

* repeat instructions following the single asterisk as directed

" inch(es)

approx approximately
beg begin/beginning
CC contrasting color
ch chain stitch
cm centimeter(s)
cn cable needle
dec decrease/decreases/decreasing
dpn(s) double-pointed needle(s)
g gram
inc increase/increases/increasing

k knit
k2tog knit 2 stitches together
LH left hand
lp(s) loop(s)
m meter(s)
M1 make one stitch
MC main color
mm millimeter(s)
oz ounce(s)
p purl
pat(s) pattern(s)
p2tog purl 2 stitches together
psso pass slipped stitch over
p2sso pass 2 slipped stitches over
rem remain/remaining
rep repeat(s)
rev St st reverse stockinette stitch
RH right hand
rnd(s) rounds
RS right side
skp slip, knit, pass stitch over—one stitch decreased

sk2p slip 1, knit 2 together, pass slip stitch over the knit 2 together—2 stitches have been decreased
sl slip
sl 1k slip 1 knitwise
sl 1p slip 1 purlwise
sl st slip stitch(es)
ssk slip, slip, knit these 2 stitches together—a decrease
st(s) stitch(es)
St st stockinette stitch/stocking stitch
tbl through back loop(s)
tog together
WS wrong side
wyib with yarn in back
wyif with yarn in front
yd(s) yard(s)
yfwd yarn forward
yo yarn over

Skill Levels

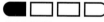

BEGINNER

Beginner projects for first-time knitters using basic stitches. Minimal shaping.

EASY

Easy projects using basic stitches, repetitive stitch patterns, simple color changes and simple shaping and finishing.

INTERMEDIATE

Intermediate projects with a variety of stitches, mid-level shaping and finishing.

EXPERIENCED

Experienced projects using advanced techniques and stitches, detailed shaping and refined finishing.

Standard Yarn Weight System
Categories of yarn, gauge ranges, and recommended needle sizes

Yarn Weight Symbol & Category Names	1 SUPER FINE	2 FINE	3 LIGHT	4 MEDIUM	5 BULKY	6 SUPER BULKY
Type of Yarns in Category	Sock, Fingering, Baby	Sport, Baby	DK, Light Worsted	Worsted, Afghan, Aran	Chunky, Craft, Rug	Bulky, Roving
Knit Gauge Range* in Stockinette Stitch to 4 inches	27–32 sts	23–26 sts	21–24 sts	16–20 sts	12–15 sts	6–11 sts
Recommended Needle in Metric Size Range	2.25–3.25mm	3.25–3.75mm	3.75–4.5mm	4.5–5.5mm	5.5–8mm	8mm and larger
Recommended Needle U.S. Size Range	1 to 3	3 to 5	5 to 7	7 to 9	9 to 11	11 and larger

* GUIDELINES ONLY: The above reflect the most commonly used gauges and needle sizes for specific yarn categories.

Inches Into Millimeters & Centimeters
All measurements are rounded off slightly.

inches	mm	cm	inches	cm	inches	cm	inches	cm
⅛	3	0.3	5	12.5	21	53.5	38	96.5
¼	6	0.6	5½	14	22	56.0	39	99.0
⅜	10	1.0	6	15.0	23	58.5	40	101.5
½	13	1.3	7	18.0	24	61.0	41	104.0
⅝	15	1.5	8	20.5	25	63.5	42	106.5
¾	20	2.0	9	23.0	26	66.0	43	109.0
⅞	22	2.2	10	25.5	27	68.5	44	112.0
1	25	2.5	11	28.0	28	71.0	45	114.5
1¼	32	3.2	12	30.5	29	73.5	46	117.0
1½	38	3.8	13	33.0	30	76.0	47	119.5
1¾	45	4.5	14	35.5	31	79.0	48	122.0
2	50	5.0	15	38.0	32	81.5	49	124.5
2½	65	6.5	16	40.5	33	84.0	50	127.0
3	75	7.5	17	43.0	34	86.5		
3½	90	9.0	18	46.0	35	89.0		
4	100	10.0	19	48.5	36	91.5		
4½	115	11.5	20	51.0	37	94.0		

Knitting Basics

Cast-On

Leaving an end about an inch long for each stitch to be cast on, make a slip knot on the right needle.

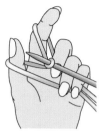

Place the thumb and index finger of your left hand between the yarn ends with the long yarn end over your thumb, and the strand from the skein over your index finger. Close your other fingers over the strands to hold them against your palm. Spread your thumb and index fingers apart and draw the yarn into a "V."

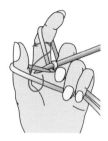

Place the needle in front of the strand around your thumb and bring it underneath this strand. Carry the needle over and under the strand on your index finger.

Draw through loop on thumb.

Drop the loop from your thumb and draw up the strand to form a stitch on the needle.

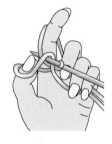

Repeat until you have cast on the number of stitches indicated in the pattern. Remember to count the beginning slip knot as a stitch.

Cable Cast-On

This type of cast-on is used when adding stitches in the middle or at the end of a row.

Make a slip knot on the left needle. Knit a stitch in this knot and place it on the left needle. Insert the right needle between the last two stitches on the left needle. Knit a stitch and place it on the left needle. Repeat for each stitch needed.

Knit (k)

Insert tip of right needle from front to back in next stitch on left needle.

Bring yarn under and over the tip of the right needle.

Pull yarn loop through the stitch with right needle point.

Slide the stitch off the left needle. The new stitch is on the right needle.

Purl (p)

With yarn in front, insert tip of right needle from back to front through next stitch on the left needle.

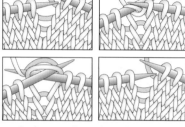

Bring yarn around the right needle counterclockwise. With right needle, draw yarn back through the stitch.

Slide the stitch off the left needle. The new stitch is on the right needle.

Bind-Off

Binding off (knit)

Knit first two stitches on left needle. Insert tip of left needle into first stitch worked on right needle and pull it over the second stitch and completely off the needle.

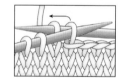

Knit the next stitch and repeat. When one stitch remains on right needle, cut yarn and draw tail through last stitch to fasten off.

Binding off (purl)

Purl first two stitches on left needle. Insert tip of left needle into first stitch worked on right needle and pull it over the second stitch and completely off the needle.

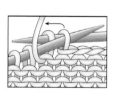

Purl the next stitch and repeat. When one stitch remains on right needle, cut yarn and draw tail through last stitch to fasten off.

Increase (inc)

Two stitches in one stitch

Increase (knit)

Knit the next stitch in the usual manner, but don't remove the stitch from the left needle. Place right needle behind left needle and knit again into the back of the same stitch. Slip original stitch off left needle.

Increase (purl)

Purl the next stitch in the usual manner, but don't remove the stitch from the left needle. Place right needle behind left needle and purl again into the back of the same stitch. Slip original stitch off left needle.

Invisible Increase (M1)

There are several ways to make or increase one stitch.

Make 1 with Left Twist (M1L)

Insert left needle from front to back under the horizontal loop between the last stitch worked and next stitch on left needle.

With right needle, knit into the back of this loop.

To make this increase on the purl side, insert left needle in same manner and purl into the back of the loop.

Make 1 with Right Twist (M1R)

Insert left needle from back to front under the horizontal loop between the last stitch worked and next stitch on left needle.

With right needle, knit into the front of this loop.

To make this increase on the purl side, insert left needle in same manner and purl into the front of the loop.

Make 1 with Backward Loop over the right needle

With your thumb, make a loop over the right needle.

Slip the loop from your thumb onto the needle and pull to tighten.

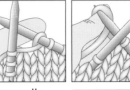

Make 1 in top of stitch below

Insert tip of right needle into the stitch on left needle one row below. Knit this stitch, then knit the stitch on the left needle.

Decrease (dec)

Knit 2 together (k2tog)

Put tip of right needle through next two stitches on left needle as to knit. Knit these two stitches as one.

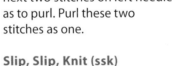

Purl 2 together (p2tog)

Put tip of right needle through next two stitches on left needle as to purl. Purl these two stitches as one.

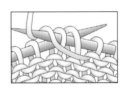

Slip, Slip, Knit (ssk)

Slip next two stitches, one at a time, as to knit from left needle to right needle.

Insert left needle in front of both stitches and work off needle together.

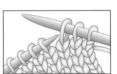

Slip, Slip, Purl (ssp)

Slip next two stitches, one at a time, as to knit from left needle to right needle. Slip these stitches back onto left needle keeping them twisted. Purl these two stitches together through back loops.

HOUSE of WHITE BIRCHES
PUBLISHERS SINCE 1947

Simple Hip Knit Scarves is published by DRG, 306 East Parr Road, Berne, IN 46711. Printed in USA. Copyright © 2010 DRG. All rights reserved. This publication may not be reproduced in part or in whole without written permission from the publisher.

RETAIL STORES: If you would like to carry this pattern book or any other DRG publications, visit DRGwholesale.com.

Every effort has been made to ensure that the instructions in this pattern book are complete and accurate. We cannot, however, take responsibility for human error, typographical mistakes or variations in individual work. Please visit AnniesCustomerCare.com to check for pattern updates.

ISBN: 978-1-59217-328-0
456789

Photo Index

37

7

9

11

14

17

19

21

25

29

27

33

39

43